STORY OF THE TITANIC

ILLUSTRATED BY STEVE NOON

WRITTEN BY DR. ERIC KENTLEY

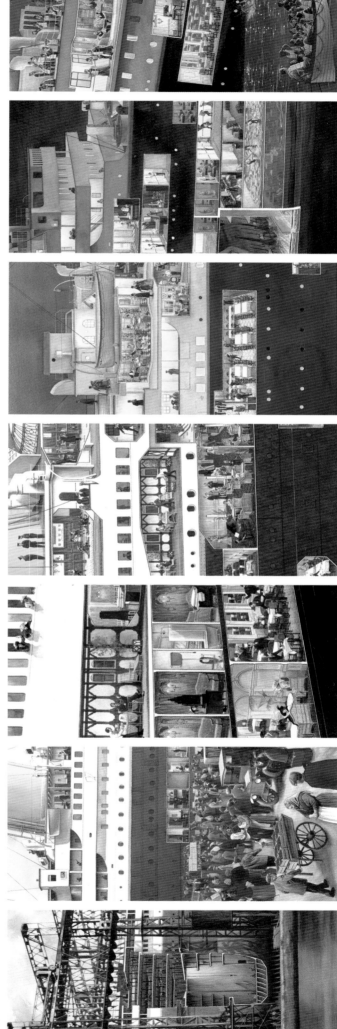

A DK Publishing Book

CONTENTS

LONDON, NEW YORK, SYDNEY, DELHI, PARIS,
MUNICH, and JOHANNESBURG

Senior Editor Linda Esposito
U.S. Editor Margaret Parrish
Senior Art Editor Diane Thistlethwaite
Jacket Designer Victoria Harvey
Production Melanie Dowland
Picture Researcher Angela Anderson
Indexer Lynn Bresler

First American Edition, 2001
01 02 03 04 05 10 9 8 7 6 5 4 3 2 1
Published in the United States by DK Publishing, Inc.
95 Madison Avenue, New York, New York 10016

Copyright © 2001 Dorling Kindersley Limited

Library of Congress Cataloging-in-Publication Data

Noon, Steve.
Story of the Titanic / Steve Noon ; illustrated by Eric Kentley.--
1st American ed.
p. cm.
ISBN 0-7894-7943-5
1. Titanic (Steamship)--Juvenile literature. 2. Shipwrecks--North
Atlantic Ocean--Juvenile literature. [1. Titanic (Steamship) 2.
Shipwrecks.] I. Kentley, Eric. Ill. II. Title.
G530.T6 N67 2001
910'.9163--dc21
2001028432

Color reproduction by Dot Gradations, UK
Printed in Malaysia by TWP Sdn Bhd

See our complete catalog at
www.dk.com

INTRODUCTION

IN THE LATE NINETEENTH AND
EARLY TWENTIETH CENTURIES,
MILLIONS OF PEOPLE EMIGRATED
FROM EUROPE TO NORTH AMERICA.

At this time, the only way across the Atlantic
was by ship – so there was great rivalry
between the shipping companies to attract as many
passengers as they could. Two of the biggest companies
were Cunard and the White Star Line. In the early
1900s, Cunard had the fastest ships. The White Star
Line decided to compete, not by concentrating on
building faster ships than Cunard, but by building new
ships that were the biggest and most luxurious in the
world. The first of these new ships to be built was the
Olympic, the second was her sister ship, the *Titanic* . . .

The *Titanic* is the most famous ship of all time, but she is
famous for the saddest of reasons. She sank on her very first
voyage, and more than 1,500 people lost their lives. Even today,
this tragedy is still one of the worst maritime disasters ever.

The *Titanic* sank because she hit an iceberg, but the people died
because she did not have enough lifeboats – and most of the
lifeboats she did have were launched half empty. The loss of life
might have been worse still if the *Titanic* had been full to
capacity – there was still room on board the ship for another
1,000 people.

THE PEOPLE WHO ARE SAILING ON THE TITANIC

More than 2,200 people are sailing on the *Titanic*'s maiden voyage. Many are 3rd-class passengers who are emigrating to America with the hope of a better way of life. This is why the *Titanic* is called "The Ship of Dreams." First-class passengers can enjoy facilities that are a match for the best hotels in the world, and even the 3rd-class accommodation on the *Titanic* and her sister ship is the equivalent of 2nd class on any other ships. These are some of the people on board. Follow their different fates as the story of the *Titanic* unfolds.

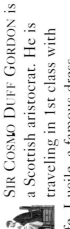

THOMAS ANDREWS is the managing director of Harland and Wolff, the company that built the *Titanic*. He is also the *Titanic*'s chief designer and knows every little detail about the ship. He is coming along on the maiden voyage to check that everything is running well and to note any changes that need to be made. He is a popular man and incredibly hardworking. He was already spent the previous week noting improvements that would make the *Titanic* even more luxurious.

EDWARD JOHN SMITH is the captain of the *Titanic*. As White Star's most experienced officer, his salary is twice that of other White Star captains. He is called the "Millionaire's Captain," because he is a favorite among society people. He has regular passengers who would not dream of crossing the Atlantic with any other captain. He has been transferred from the *Olympic*, the *Titanic*'s sister ship. This will be his last voyage. After 26 years with the company, he plans to retire.

JOSEPH BRUCE ISMAY is the managing director of the White Star Line, the *Titanic*'s owners and a company his father established. Ten years ago Bruce Ismay sold the White Star Line to an American company, but the ships still fly the British flag and have British crews. The idea to build the biggest and most luxurious ships in the world came about one evening in 1907, when Bruce Ismay went to dine with Lord Pirrie, chairman of Harland and Wolff, the *Titanic*'s builders.

AGNES SANDSTRÖM is 24. She has been visiting relatives in her native Sweden. She is now returning to the United States, where she lives with her husband in San Francisco. She is traveling in 3rd class with her 2 young daughters, Margretha (4) and Beatrice (18 months). They board the *Titanic* at Southampton, England and share a cabin with another Swedish family. Of the 497 3rd-class passengers boarding, 180 are Scandinavian.

MICHEL NAVRATIL, a tailor from France, has a secret. He is traveling under the false name of Louis Hoffman with his 2 sons, Michel (3) and Edmond (2). He is separated from his wife, but his sons stayed with him over the Easter weekend. When his wife came to pick the boys up, they had disappeared. Michel Navratil is running away with his sons to start a new life in America. They board the *Titanic* at Southampton and are traveling 2nd class.

SIR COSMO DUFF GORDON is a Scottish aristocrat. He is traveling in 1st class with his wife, Lucile, a famous dress designer for fashionable London and New York society. She has urgent business in New York and has taken the first available ship. Lady Duff Gordon's career began when her first marriage ended, leaving her penniless with a young daughter. To economize, she made most of their clothes. Friends commented on the beautiful designs, and her reputation spread.

COLONEL JOHN JACOB ASTOR is the richest 1st-class passenger of all. His fortune includes the Astoria Hotel in New York. He is also an inventor and invented a bicycle brake and a device for flattening road surfaces. Astor is returning to the United States after a long vacation with his young wife, Madeleine, who is expecting a baby. They board the *Titanic* at Cherbourg, France, with his manservant and Mrs. Astor's maid and a nurse, as well as their pet dog, Kitty.

FIFTH OFFICER HAROLD LOWE is a 28-year-old officer from Wales. He had wanted to be a sailor since he was a child, and he ran away to sea when he was 14. He had no formal education, but he earned his certificates at sea. He joined the White Star Line just 15 months ago. Before that, he spent 5 years on steamers on the coast of West Africa. This will be his first trip across the Atlantic. Lowe is a conscientious and plainspoken officer.

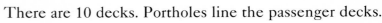

The scaffolding supporting the *Titanic* towers above surrounding buildings and can be seen from all over Belfast.

More than 2,000 steel plates are used for the hull.

BUILDING THE TITANIC

Belfast, Ireland, early in 1911

At the Harland and Wolff Shipyard more than 11,300 workers are busy building the *Titanic*. Work began 2 years ago. She is the biggest ship ever built. People call the *Titanic* "unsinkable" because of her double bottom and the added safety feature of 16 watertight compartments running across her hull.

The *Titanic's* huge rudder is higher than a 5-story building.

Thomas Andrews, the *Titanic's* chief designer, talks to Bruce Ismay, the White Star Line's managing director.

Rudder

Well for propeller

Welders

Jetty wall

SPEED IN 5 KNOTS

Timber shoring

Welder

Painters

Steam tr

4

Newly invented hydraulic machines were used to rivet many of the steel plates together.   A double bottom means that the ship is protected by a second metal "skin."

Revolving
crane

Access
ramp

Elevator

Lagan River

Portholes

Plater's shed for cutting
steel plates for hull

Decks
shored
up

E Deck

F Deck

G Deck

Space for
engine

Double bottom

Horse and cart is the main means of transport around the shipyard. It took 20 horses to carry the main anchor.   Spot two workers having a sneaky rest from work.

Thomas Andrews inspects the sumptious fixtures in a 1st-class bedroom.　Even 3rd-class accommodation has more facilities than many passengers would have at home.

A FLOATING PALACE

Belfast, Ireland, late 1911

The *Titanic* was officially launched on May 31, 1911, but she was nothing more than an empty shell. Now craftsmen are busy adorning this luxurious passenger liner with stained-glass windows, carved wood paneling, chandeliers, rich carpets, and fine furniture. Electric lighting and heating is installed, along with modern electric elevators. No expense is spared.

The squash court is just for 1st-class passengers.

Scotland Road, named after a working-class Liverpool street, is a crew's passageway that runs the length of the ship.

Painting squash court

3rd-class room

Building bunks

Scotland Road

Building bunks

Sink

3rd-class room for 6

Pullman bunk

G deck

F deck

E deck

D deck

1st-class room

Boiler uptake taking waste gas to funnel

Boiler room no. 6

Electric crane

Bridge

Carpenters

Welding

Carpets

The 1st-class rooms are furnished in different styles of period grandeur. The interior furnishings take 10 months to complete.

In all, 14 lifeboats, 2 emergency lifeboats, and 4 collapsibles are carried, enough for 1,178 people. The davits can carry twice as many boats, but this is thought unnecessary.

Twenty-nine boilers arranged in 6 boiler rooms are needed to provide the steam power for the engines. The elaborate woodwork for the Grand Staircase is carried on board.

Trimmers (whose job is to break up the coal) have separate accommodation to firemen (who feed coal into the boilers). Can you spot two firemen arguing over a bunk?

LOADING WITH SUPPLIES
Southampton, Tuesday, April 9, 1912

The *Titanic* arrived from Belfast on April 3. The quayside is bustling as she is loaded with the cargo she will carry and all the food she will need for the people on board. Families are saying their goodbyes to those of her 899 crew members still to board. Tomorrow the *Titanic* will be leaving for New York on her maiden voyage (her first trip).

The ship's larders hold 124,000 lb (56,000 kg) of meat and fish and 40,000 eggs! One crew member goes home after he gets "a funny feeling." In all, 22 crew do not sail

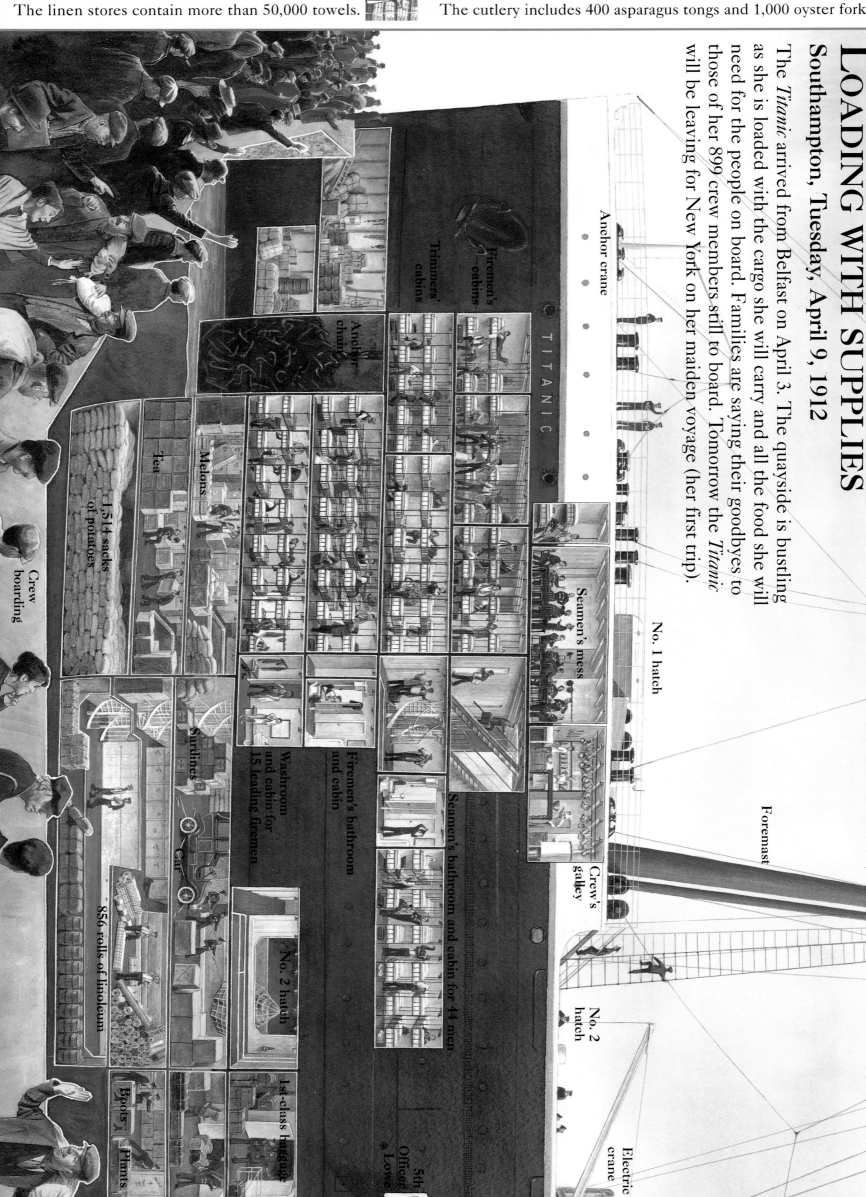

Anchor crane

Anchor

Firemen's cabins

Trimmers' cabins

Anchor chains

Melons

Tea

1,514 sacks of potatoes

Crew boarding

Sardines

Car

856 rolls of linoleum

Boots

Plants

No. 2 hatch

Washroom and cabin for 15 leading firemen

Firemen's bathroom and cabin

Seamen's bathroom and cabin for 44 men

Seamen's mess

Crew's galley

No. 1 hatch

Foremast

No. 2 hatch

Electric crane

5th Officer Lowe

1st-class baggage

TITANIC

Thomas Andrews
inspecting lifeboats

No. 8 lifeboat

No. 6 lifeboat

No. 4 lifeboat

Collapsible B

No. 2
emergency
lifeboat

5th Officer
(Lowe)

3rd
Officer

6th
Officer

Boat deck

Captain Smith
on the bridge

Port light

A deck

B deck

C deck

D deck

E deck

Bosun

Ship's
carpenter

Quartermasters
(6)

Stewards'
lavatory

Dishwashers
(20)

2nd-class
stewards (42)

Beer wagon

ALES &

Quayside
(cutaway)

Photographer

Who's this sneaking a drink?    After the 2 promenade suites, the 2 parlor suites are the most expensive on board.

THE PASSENGERS BOARD

Southampton, Wednesday, April 10, 10:30 am

Passengers have been boarding all morning. A boat train from London's Waterloo station arrived at 9:30 am, carrying 2nd- and 3rd-class passengers. Another, carrying 1st-class passengers, is due at 11:30 am. At midday the *Titanic* will set sail.

Bruce Ismay's promenade suite has its own private promenade

Parlor suite

Sitting room

Bedroom

Lavatory

Bathroom

Bedroom

A steward serves Bruce Ismay tea

1st-class bedroom

1st-class bedroom

Captain Smith

1st-class reception

1st-class dining saloon

Stewards preparing for lunch

Engine

Captain Smith greets 1st-class passengers in the reception room.

Titanic's largest room is its 1st-class dining saloon. Styled on a 17th-century stately home, it seats 550

Many 1st-class passengers bring their own servants. A 2nd-class passenger calling himself Louis Hoffman boards with his 2 sons. This Frenchman's real name is Navratil.

Agnes Sandström and her 2 daughters are returning 3rd class to the US after a vacation in Sweden.

board are 7,000 lettuce heads and 6,615 lb (3,000 kg) of tomatoes.

Docking bridge

Poop deck

Michel Navatril and his sons

2nd-class room

3rd-class room

2nd-class entrance

3rd-class entrance

Palm Court

1st-class smoking room

1st-class promenade

Thomas Andrews

Baker

1st-class rooms

Maid

Engineers' mess

Stewards carrying luggage

1st-class bedrooms

Kitchen

Scotland Road

Cook

The trip from Southampton to Ireland costs 1st-class passengers £4 ($19.50.)

The ship-to-shore journey takes half an hour.

The blue ensign is flying because Captain Smith belongs to the British Royal Naval Reserve.

LEAVING THE LAST PORT OF CALL

Ireland, Thursday, April 11, 1912

After a brief stop at Cherbourg in France, where many wealthy Americans boarded after spending the social season in Europe, the *Titanic* arrived in Queenstown (now Cobh). She was too big to dock in the port and had to anchor more than 1.8 miles (3 km) offshore instead. A few passengers disembarked, but another 120 joined the ship, and 1,385 sacks of mail were loaded. Just after 1:30 pm, after a stay of only 2 hours, the *Titanic* sets sail for New York.

The flag of the White Star Line shows the distinctive company logo.

A White Star tender takes passengers disembarking from the *Titanic* to shore.

One of the crew deserts ship: he lives in Queenstown and used the *Titanic* as a free trip home.

12

Can you spot Captain Smith?   Millionaire John Jacob Astor bought a lace shawl from a boat for his pregnant wife.

This is a dummy funnel, used as a ventilator rather than a chimney.   The *Titanic*'s owners thought that 4 funnels were more impressive than the 3 actually needed.

Small boats with Irish linen, lace, and other souvenirs for sale went to the ship.

The US flag is flying because White Star was bought by a US company in 1902.

The wind has taken a lady's hat. Can you spot where it is? Between 1 pm and 3 pm the gymnasium is open to children only. It has all the most up-to-date equipmen

RELAXING AT SEA

Sunday, April 14, 2:15 pm

A few days into the voyage, passsengers are relaxing and making use of the ship's facilities. The different classes walk on separate promenades, talk in separate lounges, and eat in separate dining rooms. The swimming pool, gymnasium, and Turkish baths are for the exclusive use of 1st-class passengers.

Serving tea

1st-class promenade

1st-class lounge

1st-class dining saloon

1st-class dining saloon

3rd-class dining room

Children playing hoops

Reading and Writing Room

Hobby horse

The Duff Gordons enjoy a 4-course luncheon in the 1st-class dining saloon.

The Sandströms' lunch is called "dinner." Choice is limited, but the portions are generou

The 2 promenade suites on B deck have private promenades and are the most expensive at $4,230.   Bruce Ismay receives a wireless message warning of ice ahead.

Collapsible A

No. 3 lifeboat

No. 5 lifeboat

Bruce Ismay

Glass dome

1st-class entrance and Grand Staircase

Enclosed 1st-class promenade

Electric elevator

Grand Staircase

Heated salt-water pool

Turkish baths' cooling room

Mosaic floor

5th Officer Lowe

Rowing machines

Gymnasium

Private promenade

1st-class reception room

deck

deck

deck

deck

deck

Topped with a glass dome to let in natural light, the ornately carved Grand Staircase is the *Titanic's* crowning glory.   The Turkish baths are decorated in "Arabian" style.

There are so many dogs on board that a dog show is planned for April 15.

The temperature is just above freezing. People taking the air are dressed warmly.

DINING ON BOARD
Sunday, April 14, 8:50 pm

This evening, 1st-class passengers can enjoy an 11-course feast in the dining saloon, 2nd-class passengers can choose fish, chicken, or lamb as part of their 3-course meal, while beef stew, bread, and tea are served in 3rd class. After eating, the more hardy take an evening stroll, but the temperature has dropped 10 degrees in 2 hours. Captain Smith is worried about ice and calls in at the bridge before going to bed at 9.20 pm.

3rd-class general room

Steward walking dogs on poop deck

Electric cranes

3rd-class promenade

2nd-class promenade

2nd-class promenade

2nd-class dining saloon

2nd-class promenade

Main mast

Electric cranes

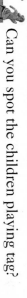

Can you spot the children playing tag?

In the 2nd-class dining saloon, Mr. Navratil and his sons attend hymn singing. Many hymns are about dangers at sea.

After dinner, Andrews returns to his cabin to continue working. Tonight the Atlantic is very calm, like a glass lake.

Captain Smith leaves a party in his honor in the À la Carte Restaurant.

n the evening, the Verandah Café becomes a playroom for young 1st-class passengers.

The Café Parisien is a copy of a sidewalk café in Paris and has genuine French waiters.

le 1st-class passengers take an after-dinner drink in the smoking room.

Who are these men playing cards?

If the ship had turned to port at full speed, she would have missed the iceberg.

Obeying 1st Officer Murdoch's orders, Quartermaster Hichens has swung the wheel as far as he can.

Sixth Officer Moody notes the time of collision in the ship's log.

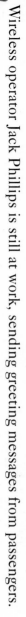

Wireless operator Jack Phillips is still at work, sending greeting messages from passengers.

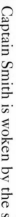

Captain Smith is woken by the sound of the iceberg scraping along the hull.

No. 5 lifeboat

Marconi room

1st-class promenade

No. 3 lifeboat

Collapsible A

Captain Smith

No. 1 emergency lifeboat

Bridge

Wheelhouse

Morse lamp

Starboard light

ICEBERG AHEAD!
Sunday, April 14, 11:40 pm

In the crow's nest 2 lookouts are scanning the sea for ice. Suddenly a massive iceberg looms ahead. They ring the alarm bell and telephone the bridge. First Officer Murdoch gives the order to reverse the engines and steer the ship to port (left). He saves the ship from a head-on collision, but the iceberg scrapes along the side of the ship, cutting long slices into the hull below the waterline.

Forecastle deck

Firemen

Trimmers

Greasers

Firemen's mess

3rd class

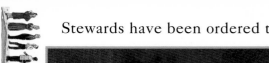

The Duff Gordons wait in the gym to escape the cold. People still believe the ship is unsinkable.

Fifth Officer Lowe and crewmen take the covers off the lifeboats.

Passengers line up outside the purser's office for their valuables.

The bulkheads go up to E deck – the watertight doors can't stop water from flowing over the top

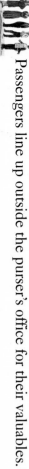

Gymnasium

5th Officer Lowe

Reception room

Steward

1st class promenade

1st class

Purser's office

Grand Staircase

Steward

BULKHEAD

Coal

Coal

Boiler
room
no. 5

1st class

No. 1 funnel

1st class

BULKHEAD

Boiler
room
no. 6

3rd class

1st class

Bridge and
wheelhouse

Arguing over way out

BULKHEAD

Mail sacks

Post office

3rd class

1st class

Young passengers play football with ice on the well deck.   Thomas Andrews and Captain Smith take just 10 minutes to assess that the damage is enough to sink the ship.

THE *TITANIC* IS DOOMED
Sunday, April 14, midnight

Captain Smith calls Thomas Andrews to the bridge, and the 2 men make a quick tour of the ship. The first 5 compartments are filling with water fast, pulling down the bow. It is clear to Andrews that the ship will sink in a few hours. Captain Smith gives the order to uncover the lifeboats.

Crow's nest

3rd class

E deck

1st-class baggage

Captain Smith

Andrews

3rd class

3rd class

Cargo

Cargo

BULKHEAD

BULKHEAD

Cargo

Cargo

The iceberg has cut gashes in the hull over 328 ft (100 m) in length, and water is flooding in.   Some 3rd-class passengers can't find a way to the boat deck.

Mr. Navratil searches for a lifeboat to save his sons.

Spot the distant light. If it is another ship, it does not respond.

The ship's baker throws deckchairs overboard, which he and others might be able to use as life rafts.

The band plays waltz and ragtime tunes to keep up everyone's spirits.

Thomas Andrews urges passengers to get into the lifeboats.

An officer fires his gun to stop passengers from storming a lifeboat after some men are forcibly removed.

No. 3 funnel

No. 3 lifeboat

Heading for stern

Lounge

Baker

2 boats remain on port side

1st-class dining saloon

E deck

Reception room

Thomas Andrews

Gymnasium

No. 2 funnel

Band play on port side

Grand Staircase

Parting from father

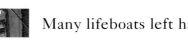
The wireless operators send out distress signals to other ships. It is the first time a ship uses the new signal "SOS."   Rockets are fired to alert any ships in the area.

THE LAST LIFEBOATS
Monday, 15 April, 1:10 am

The *Titanic* is sinking fast, and it is now clear that there are not enough lifeboats for all those left on board. The order is "women and children first", but many of the lifeboats have already been launched just half full. The wireless operators have been sending out distress signals to ships in the area – the only hope left is that one can reach the *Titanic* before she sinks.

Bridge

An officer fires distress rockets

Captain Smith

The Astors search for a lifeboat

Bow below water

No. 1 emergency lifeboat

No. 1 funnel

Collapsible A

Bruce Ismay

Collapsible C

Men taken off boat

Saying goodbye

Marconi room

B deck

G deck

D deck

23

As collapsible lifeboat C starts its descent, Bruce Ismay steps in.   Captain Smith orders the lifeboats to stand by, ready to return to pick up people from the water.

THE FINAL MOMENTS

Monday, April 15, 2:18 am

All the lifeboats have gone. No ship has been able to reach the *Titanic* in time. The crowd of people on the stern have no hope of rescue now. As the bow sinks further and further, the stern is lifted higher and higher out of the water. Suddenly a huge roar is heard as the ship breaks in two. In a few moments the *Titanic*'s lights will go out. The stern will rise until it is completely upright – then slide out of sight into the icy water.

Collapsible C

Collapsible B

No. 4 lifeboat

Collapsible D

People balance on upturned collapsible B, which was washed off the deck before it could be launched.

People won't survive more than half an hour in the freezing water.

Mrs. Astor is in no. 4 lifeboat, but her husband was refused a place.

The Navratil brothers are in collapsible D, the last boat to leave. Their father is still on the ship.

The ship's baker stands at the stern. Frightened of being sucked down by the sinking ship, the lifeboats pull away.

Officer Lowe, in no. 14 lifeboat, is the only one to go back after the sinking to try to rescue people from the water.

Thomas Andrews is last seen in the smoking room.

No. 13 lifeboat   No. 14 lifeboat

No. 8 lifeboat

A man checks the time. At 2:20 am the *Titanic* sinks – just 2 hours and 40 minutes after striking the iceberg.

Mrs. Sandström and her daughters are safe in no. 13 lifeboat.

Daylight shows the survivors that they are in the middle of an icefield.

Commanded by Captain Rostron, the *Carpathia* is a British ship belonging to the Cunard Line.

Carpathia's passengers watch the rescue.

Survivors who clung to collapsible B were picked up by lifeboats 4 and 12.

THE SURVIVORS ARE RESCUED

Monday, April 15, about 6:30 am

The *Carpathia*, on her way from New York to Gibraltar, received the distress call from the *Titanic* just after midnight. Immediately, the *Carpathia's* captain changed course and sped as fast as he could toward the stricken ship, dodging icebergs all the way. But the *Carpathia* was 53 miles (93 km) away and could not reach the site until 3:35 am. At 4:10 am, no. 2 emergency lifeboat was alongside and being unloaded. One by one, the others followed, but it was not until after 8:00 am that the last survivors boarded. In all, 706 people were rescued by the *Carpathia*.

No. 4 lifeboat

No. 9 lifeboat

A seaman helps row no. 4 lifeboat. He doesn't know that his pay – like that of all the *Titanic* crew – stopped at midnight.

Like many survivors, Mrs. Astor is now a widow.

S.S. TITANIC
4

Bruce Ismay climbs on board.

Fortified by alcohol, the ship's baker survived 2 hours in the sea before he was rescued.

No. 1 lifeboat, with the Duff Gordons on board, is the second boat to be rescued.

Able survivors climb rope ladders to enter the ship. The less able are winched on board.

No. 13 lifeboat

No. 1 emergency lifeboat

Collapsible C

CARPATHIA

Collapsible D

No. 14 lifeboat

Fifth Officer Lowe sails no. 14 lifeboat to the *Carpathia* with collapsible D in tow.

The *Carpathia's* crew is ready with blankets, food, and medical help for the survivors.

FIRST NEWS OF THE SINKING

Many ships in the North Atlantic had heard the *Titanic*'s distress call, and as the morning of April 15 progressed several arrived on the scene to see if they could help. But it was too late. No other survivors were found.

At 8:50 am the *Carpathia* set off for New York. Her wireless operator worked around the clock to let anxious relatives know who had been saved. Bruce Ismay dictated a telegram to notify the White Star Line that the *Titanic* had sunk with a serious loss of life, but *Carpathia*'s operator did not send this until April 17.

The *Carpathia* sets sail for New York.

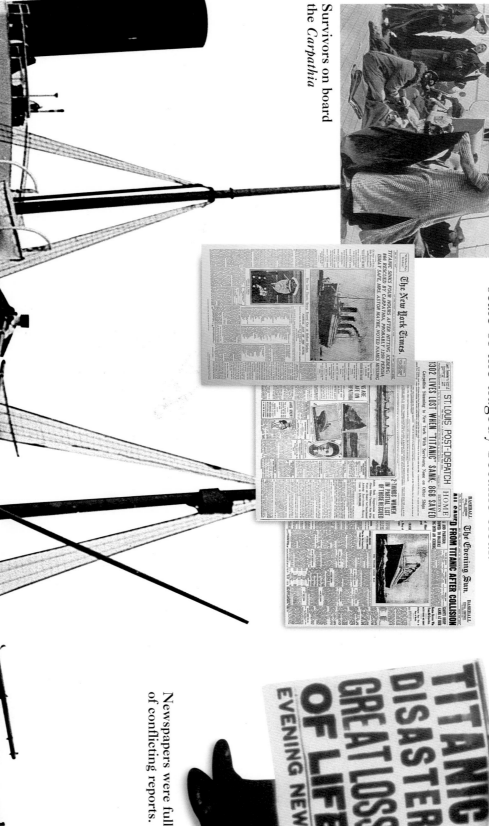

Survivors on board the *Carpathia*

However, the *Titanic*'s distress calls had alerted the world. First newspaper reports stated that the *Titanic* was being towed into Halifax in Canada, but by April 16 it was clear that this was a major disaster. Slowly, as telegrams from the *Carpathia* gave the names of the survivors, the horrific scale of the tragedy became clear.

Newspapers were full of conflicting reports.

TITANIC DISASTER GREAT LOSS OF LIFE
EVENING NEWS

SURVIVORS ARRIVE IN AMERICA

When the *Carpathia* sailed into New York at 8 pm on April 18, 1912, there was a crowd of 40,000 people waiting for her. Among them were the friends and relatives of those who had sailed on the *Titanic*. Confused by the differing newspaper reports, they were frantic for news. But it was another hour before the survivors began to disembark. First, the *Carpathia* dropped off the *Titanic*'s lifeboats at the White Star pier before berthing at Cunard's pier.

First to disembark were the 1st-class passengers. Madeleine Astor, still accompanied by her nurse and a maid, was met by her stepson and whisked away in a car. Many 3rd-class passengers had lost everything in the disaster. However, the White Star Line helped by providing temporary shelter for them.

Harold McBride, the only surviving wireless operator, is carried off the *Carpathia* with frostbitten feet.

Spotlights illuminated the crowd so that the survivors might have a chance of seeing friends and relatives. The crowd was swelled by members of the press, who were in search of a good story and ruthlessly hassled survivors. But many refused to speak about the disaster. The night of the *Titanic*'s sinking would haunt them for the rest of their lives.

As hope faded of finding their loved ones among the survivors, many in the waiting throng became hysterical with grief.

THE INQUIRIES

Bruce Ismay is quizzed at the American inquiry.

Two inquiries were held into the loss of the *Titanic*, one in the United States and one in England. The hearings lasted a total of 17 days. The American inquiry was very critical of Captain Smith, questioning why a ship under his command was going so fast through an ice field at night. This question is still unanswered. But there was also evidence that the *Titanic*'s crew had not been properly drilled to launch the lifeboats.

Another line of questioning referred to the *Californian*, a ship that the inquiries said was near enough to the *Titanic* to have been able to rescue everyone on board, but remained motionless all night because of the ice. The *Californian*'s wireless operator did not hear the *Titanic*'s call for help because he went off duty. The captain was accused of failing to act when he saw distress rockets, although his crew testified that the rockets came from a much smaller ship than the *Titanic*. Many on board the *Titanic* reported seeing the lights of another ship, too close to have been the *Californian*. This has led to the theory that there was a third, mystery ship in the area that night.

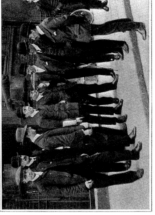

The *Californian*'s crew at the British inquiry

Claims that 3rd-class passengers were prevented from reaching the lifeboats were not proved. But gates separating the 3 classes had remained closed. Also, the fact that many 3rd-class passengers did not speak English had added to the confusion and made escape difficult.

Some good did come out of the disaster. Outdated regulations that required so few lifeboats on board were severely criticized. It quickly became compulsory to have lifeboat space for every person on board a ship. It also became compulsory for the wireless to be operated around the clock, and an International Ice Patrol was established.

WHAT HAPPENED TO THE PEOPLE?

The sinking of the *Titanic* took many lives and devastated a great many others. Families were split apart. Many of the women and children who survived left husbands and fathers behind – and never saw them again. This is what happened to the people we have followed through the book.

Captain Smith

There are many stories about the fate of **Captain Smith**. Some survivors said they had seen him in the water. Others said he shot himself. The most reliable witnesses reported that he stayed on the bridge and went down with his ship.

Thomas Andrews knew better than anyone else how quickly the *Titanic* would sink. He encouraged as many people as he could to put on their lifejackets and get into the lifeboats. But his last moments are a mystery. A steward saw him standing alone in the 1st-class smoking room and said that he made no attempt to save himself. Others said they had seen him on the boat deck, throwing deckchairs to people in the water so they could use them as floats.

Thomas Andrews

Bruce Ismay helped passengers into the lifeboats. But, as half-empty collapsible C was being lowered, he stepped into it. This was seen as a cowardly act, and his reputation was ruined. During the inquiries he was quizzed about reports that he had ordered Captain Smith to sail at top speed, despite the danger of icebergs. Ismay denied this, claiming he had no authority over a captain and his ship.

Bruce Ismay

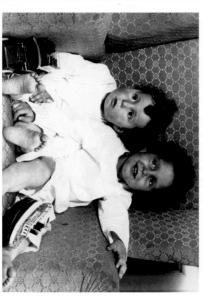

Michel Navratil managed to get his sons into the last lifeboat that left the *Titanic*, but he did not survive himself. Pictures of the two French boys, dubbed "the orphans of the *Titanic*," were published all over the world. In Nice, Marcelle Navratil recognized them as her kidnapped sons and sailed immediately to be reunited with them.

Michel (right) and Edmond Navratil

Colonel Astor asked if he could accompany his wife in the lifeboat because of her delicate condition. But when he was refused, he stepped politely back. His body was recovered from the sea. **Madeleine Astor's** baby son was born in August 1912 and named after his father.

Lady Duff Gordon

Sir Cosmo Duff Gordon was interrogated very closely at the British inquiry. It was rumored that he had bribed members of the crew not to return to save the drowning because he feared their boat would be swamped. He was cleared, but his reputation was ruined. **Lady Duff Gordon** thrived on the publicity and opened a new shop in Paris later that year.

Fifth Officer Harold Lowe reached the rank of commander in the Royal Naval Reserve, but he never became a captain in the merchant service – nor did any other officer who survived the sinking of the *Titanic*.

Agnes Sandström and her daughters were reunited with her husband in the United States, but they returned to live in Sweden when he died some years later.

Fifth Officer Lowe

The Astors

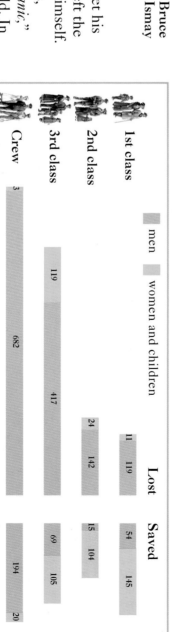

	Lost		Saved	
	men	women and children	men	women and children
1st class	119	11	54	145
2nd class	142	24	15	104
3rd class	417	119	69	105
Crew	682	3	194	20

The White Star Line did not have a proper passenger list, so even to this day there are arguments among historians about the precise number of people who died. The American inquiry stated that 1,517 were lost and 706 survived, while the British inquiry put the number of deaths at 1,490. This graph is based on the figures of the American inquiry. The numbers show a big difference between the 3 classes.

SEARCH FOR THE TITANIC

Recovered objects: playing cards, cherub from the Grand Staircase, and a letter.

Plans to find and recover the *Titanic* began immediately after the sinking. But the water in the North Atlantic was too deep. The *Titanic* had sunk to over 13,000 ft (4,000 m) – more than 10 times the height of the Empire State Building. The technology did not exist to go down to those depths until the late 1970s.

In 1985, a joint US/French expedition, led by Dr. Robert Ballard, began a detailed search of the area, using an unmanned submersible equipped with video cameras. On September 1, after weeks searching the murky depths, the video monitor showed an image of one of the *Titanic*'s single-ended boilers. The ship had been found! She was more than 12 miles (20 km) away from her last recorded position.

The *Titanic* had broken in half as she sank, and the bow and the stern were almost a mile apart. Much of the ship's contents – crockery, bottles, luggage, even sinks and floor tiles – had spilled out over an area, known as the debris field, over a mile square.

Serving platter

Ballard returned to the wreck site the following year with a submersible and traveled down to the seabed to see the ship. He also published the coordinates of the *Titanic*'s position.

The *Titanic* is a wreck in international waters – she has no protection as an historic wreck. As a result, there was a race among salvagers to get to the site as quickly as possible and stake a claim. But there were very few submersibles in the world capable of working at that depth. In 1987, the French organization that had worked with Ballard teamed up with another American company. The manned submersible *Nautile* went down to the wreck and, using the vessel's mechanical arms, retrieved hundreds of objects from the site. The expedition caused a storm of protest. Some saw it as no better than grave robbing. However, the company has been working the site ever since and has raised several thousand artifacts from the debris field. It has loaned these artifacts to exhibitions on both sides of the Atlantic.

The Nautile is transported to the wreck site.

GLOSSARY

À la carte restaurant A restaurant that has no set meal. Diners can choose whatever they would like from the menu.

Boat deck The deck where the lifeboats are stored.

Boiler A large furnace where coal is burned to boil water. The steam produced powers the ship.

Bosun An officer who looks after a ship's boats and flags.

Bow The front end of a ship.

Bridge The control center of a ship from which she is navigated.

Bulkhead A solid wall to stop fire or flooding.

Bunk A narrow bed fixed along a wall or one above another.

Cabin A room on a ship where passengers sleep.

Collapsible A lifeboat with canvas sides that collapse for easy storage.

Crow's nest A lookout platform high up on the foremast.

Davit One of a pair of cranes, equipped with pulleys and ropes, by which lifeboats are lowered.

Ensign A flag distinguishing a nation or service.

Fireman A person who feeds the ship's boilers with coal.

Forecastle A short raised deck at the front of a ship.

Foremast The mast nearest the front of a ship.

Funnel A tall chimney from which smoke escapes.

Gangway A passageway into a ship.

Greaser A semiskilled worker who attends to a ship's engines.

Hull The main body of a ship.

Hydraulic machine One that works by using the pressure of liquids, usually water or oil.

Lifejacket A device to keep a person afloat in the water.

Log A detailed record of a ship's voyage.

Marconi room Wireless operators worked here, using a system devised by Guglielmo Marconi.

Mess room A place where a ship's crew eat and relax.

Morse lamp A lamp used to transmit messages by flashing the light.

Poop deck A raised deck at the stern of a ship.

Port The left-hand side of a ship, looking forward.

Porthole A small, usually round, window in the side of a ship.

Promenade A deck area for passengers to walk and take the sea air.

Propeller A device with angled blades that turn in the water and move a ship forward.

Purser An officer who keeps a ship's accounts.

Quartermaster An officer in charge of steering a ship and other navigational duties.

Quay A platform next to the water for loading and unloading ships.

Ragtime A style of jazz popular in the early 1900s.

Rivet A short metal bolt that fastens two pieces of metal together.

Rudder A vertical device at the rear of a ship used for steering.

Saloon The name for a large public room on a ship.

Shoring A set of props used to support a structure.

Starboard The right-hand side of a ship, looking forward.

Stern The rear end of a ship.

Steward/stewardess A person who looks after the passengers.

Suite Connected rooms.

Tender A boat that carries things between a larger ship and shore.

Trimmer A person who breaks up large lumps of coal for the boilers.

Turkish bath A steam bath.

Well deck Part of an upper deck of a ship enclosed by bulkheads supporting higher decks.

Wireless An old word for radio.

INDEX

The publisher would like to thank the following for their kind permission to reproduce their photographs:

a=above, c=center, b=below, l=left, r=right, t=top
Corbis: 29tr, 29b, 29b, 30bl, 31b; 30tr; Mary Evans Picture Library: 28tc. 28ct. 29tc. Illustrated London News Picture Library: 29c. Popperfoto: 30cl. Rex Features: 02–3t, 28c. 29tr, 31tr, 31cl, 31t; Nils Jorgansen 31tr; Topham Picturepoint: 30c. 30cr, 31c. 31c.

Steve Noon would like to thank the Ulster Folk and Transport Museum Picture Library for its help with the illustrations on pages 4–7.